# ARTEMIS AND THE ARTEMISION

# ARTEMIS
## AND THE ARTEMISION

### THE MYSTERY CENTRE AT EPHESUS

Peter Stebbing

Anthroposophical Publications

Cover design by Peter Stebbing & Urs Rüd
Cover illustration: A column base from the late classical Artemision, British Museum
(Photo: *P.St.*)

ISBN: 978-1-948302-18-0 Paperback


Anthroposophical Publications
Part of The e.Lib, Inc.
Visit the website at https://AnthroposophicalPublications.org/

Printed in the United States of America

*Great epochs in art, epochs in which eminent artistic achievements come into being, ever and again derive their artistic sources from initiation. In this way, art introduces spiritual life into physical life.*

Rudolf Steiner, 30th January 1915

The area surrounding the ruins of the Artemision, seen from the south.
To the right the column erected in 1972 (14 m) upon which storks nest in spring. In the background
the Isa Bey Mosque, the citadel and the ruins of the early Christian Basilica of St. John.

View looking southwest from a point on the Ayasoluk hill.
The site of the Artemision is marked as above by a single column seen here in the middle of the picture.
*Ortygia* and the "House of Mary" are located to the left in the wooded hills beyond. (Photo: *P. St.*)

# Artemis and the Artemision

## The Mystery Centre at Ephesus

*Behold the Logos*
*In the scorching fire:*
*Find the solution*
*In Diana's House*

Rudolf Steiner, GA 232

## *Peter Stebbing*

Among the Seven Wonders of the World, the Hellenes counted the Egyptian pyramids, the Tower of Babel, the Temple of the Ephesian Artemis, the enormous gold and ivory image of Zeus of Olympia, the Lighthouse of Alexandria, the Colossus of Rhodes and the Mausoleum of Halicarnassus.

With the ruins of the Artemis temple almost non-existent today, it is perhaps not surprising that little interest is generally accorded this 6th Wonder of the World. Yet we can still gain an idea of it and of the legendary statue of Artemis, from reconstruction drawings and archaeological finds – supported by literary and historical sources (Herodotus, Pliny the Elder, Pausanias).

### The First, Archaic Artemision

The ancient Greeks asked: Why was the goddess Artemis unable to protect her own "house," the Artemision, from destruction? The Ephesians are known to have responded, "She was not in Ephesus on the night the Temple burnt down, but in Pella (the original capital city of Macedonia) assisting at the birth of Alexander." The historical facts are well-known. The fire in the Temple of Artemis, the act of a certain *Herostratus,* took place on the 6th of February in the year 356 B.C., the night Alexander the Great was born to Olympias and Philip II of Macedon.

There is evidence that a sacred precinct had existed on the site of the Sanctuary of Artemis as far back as the 9th century B.C. In the second half of the 8th century a small wooden temple fronted on all sides with columns, measuring no more than 13,5 x 6,5 meters, was built on the site that later became the inner courtyard of the subsequent monumental marble temple. It had 8 x 4 wooden columns and an open *cella*, the sacred inner chamber. Of these columns, only the green slate bases remain. Evidence of a tile roof was discovered in 1994. This small wooden temple housed a wooden statue personifying Artemis and already anticipates the Ionic monumental temple (see ground plan). It is the oldest

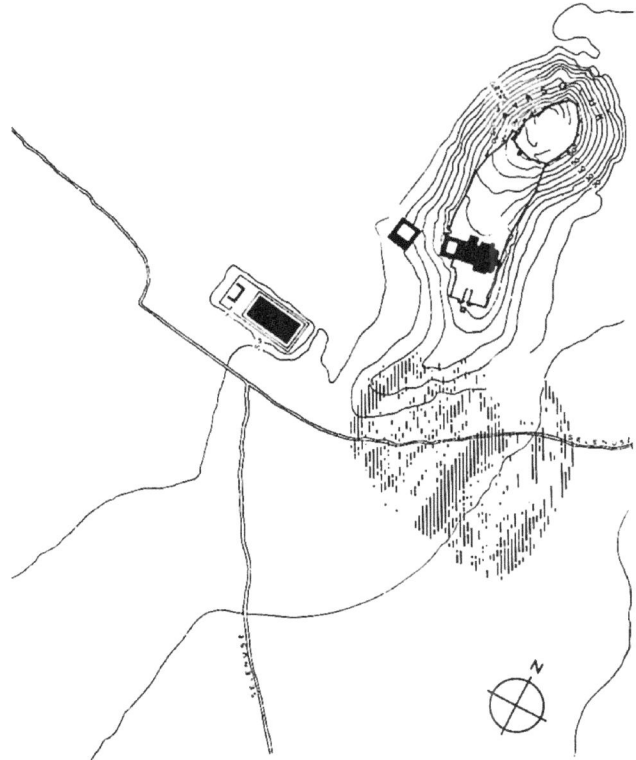

Map showing the site of the Artemision and the location of the nearby (unexcavated) archaic-classical Greek settlement of Ephesus (shaded area). The Basilica of St. John was built close by on the Ayasoluk hill in the mid 6th century A.D. on the site of his tomb, partly using stones from the ruins of the Artemision. Numerous marble columns of the temple were also transported to Constantinople in building the Haga-Sophia Basilica.

As little more than the site itself remains of the Temple of Artemis, this is for the most part an invisible monument. (Long forgotten and unknown, even the approximate actual site of the Artemision remained a mystery until its discovery on New Year's day 1870 by John Turtle Wood, an English railway engineer and architect, after an arduous seven-year search.)

known example of post-Mycenaean Greek architecture and dates approximately from the time of Homer.

The tomb of St. John, within the Basilica of St. John on the Ayasoluk hill. (Photo: *P. St.*)

King Croesus, the fabulously rich and powerful ruler of the Lydians, gained influence in Ephesus, having laid siege to the city. He bequeathed immense sums for the building of the Artemision, begun as a great marble temple during his reign (560–546 B.C.), decreeing at the same time a new layout of the original Greek city of Ephesus at the foot of the Ayasoluk hill (see map). To this day, this settlement remains unexcavated, unlike the renovated Hellenistic-Roman "New Ephesus" (initially called Arsinoëia) situated 3 km to the southwest. (A refounding of the city became necessary in 296 B.C. due to rising ground waters, an outcome of changing sea levels during the 4th century B.C.)

The archaic Artemision begun by Croesus differs from other Greek temples in that it was conceived on a much larger scale, with twenty columns on the long sides and eight on the west front, each almost 20 meters in height – as compared to 10,25 meters for the columns of the Parthenon. The Cretan *Chersiphron*, his son *Metagenes* and *Theodoros of Samos* were the architects of this *dipteros* – a temple with a surrounding double row of columns – laid out on an east-west axis. By one account – though this would seem improbable – the Ionic columns were all of *one piece* and not made up of individual marble drums. The twenty-eight sculptural column bases instituted by Croesus occur nowhere else in Greece. The admiration shown for the artistic and technological achievement in building this unique temple is reflected in the legend that the lintel of the great door was put in place by the goddess Artemis herself. It was just under sixty meters wide, as compared to seventy meters for the *length* of the Parthenon in Athens – a scale characteristic of Egyptian temples. Hence, the Artemision may in a sense be regarded as representing a transition from one cultural epoch to another. In the words of Rudolf Steiner:

*"The Mystery of Ephesus stood midway between the ancient Oriental Mysteries and the Greek Mysteries. It held a unique position. For, in Ephesus those who attained to initiation were still able to experience something of the tremendous majestic truths of the ancient East. Their souls were still stirred with a deep inward experience of the connection of the human being with the Macrocosm."* [1]

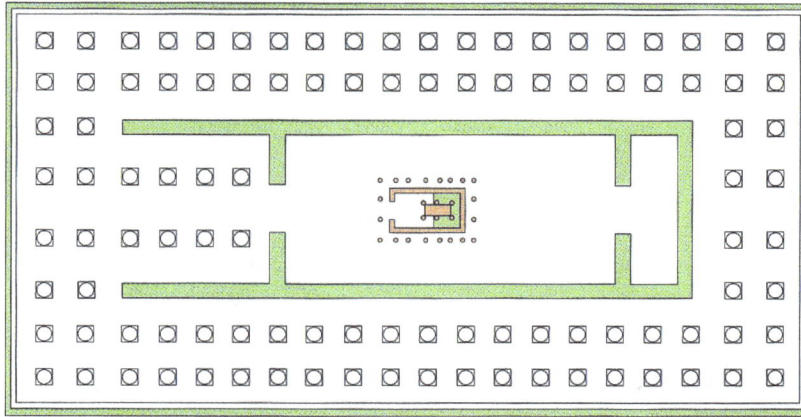

Ground plan of the archaic Artemision (mid 6ᵗʰ century B.C., *green*);
with early cult buildings, such as the small *peripteros* temple with
baldachin for the cult statue (8ᵗʰ century B.C., *pink*). Archeologists are in
agreement that the west front had no more than two rows of columns.

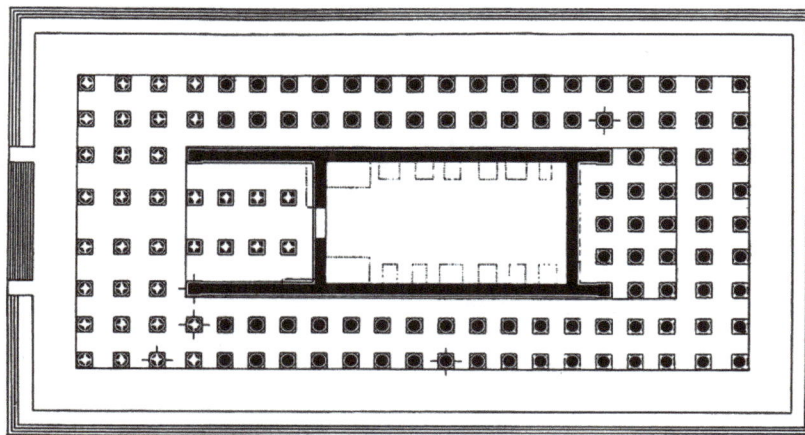

Late classical Artemision. 36 column bases of the west entrance hall had
relief sculptures. Reconstruction drawing *Fritz Krischen*, 1933.

Situated on the Anatolian coast facing toward the Greek peninsula across the Aegean, the Artemision contrasted with other Greek temples in facing west, rather than to the east. The various statues of Artemis that have survived resemble oriental and Egyptian cult figures in their strictly frontal, upright posture.

Given its monumental proportions, it would seem almost completely inexplicable that such an immense stone structure could have been destroyed by fire. It is said, however, to have had cedar-wood beams and a coffered ceiling with doors of cypress-wood. The historical reports of this fire are duly confirmed by archeologists, in that the remaining column stumps of the archaic temple reveal traces of it.

The young Alexander arrived in Ephesus in 334 B.C.,

following his defeat of the Persians in a battle on the river Granicus [Kocabas]. His army paraded in honour of Artemis, but the Ephesians declined his offer of help in rebuilding the temple. In contrast to the commonly held view that the adventures of Alexander were motivated by the urge for conquest, Rudolf Steiner indicates that:

"*Alexander, on the day of whose birth the physical Ephesus had fallen, resolved to found a spiritual Ephesus that should send its Sun-rays far out into East and West. It was in very truth this purpose that lay at the root of all he undertook: to found a spiritual Ephesus, reaching out across Asia Minor eastwards to India, covering also Egyptian Africa and the East of Europe.*" [2]

Model of the second (late classical) Artemision.
The cult-image was housed in a *naiskos* (a small temple-like building) within the *sekos*
(open court area) toward the eastern end. Ephesus Museum, Selçuk, Turkey. (Photo *P.St.*)

## The Second, Classical Artemision

*Paionios*, *Demetrios* and *Cheirokrates* are known to have been the architects of the rebuilding, on the same site. Due to the increased groundwater, a terrace was built over the foundations of the archaic temple: a 2,76 meter high platform on which the new temple was to stand. [3] All essential elements of the archaic temple were retained, including columns with reliefs by renowned sculptors, such as *Praxiteles* (370–330 B.C.). [4] Begun around 336 B.C., the second Artemision was completed during the latter part of the 4th century, and stood for almost 600 years, being partially destroyed by an earth-quake in the year 262 A.D. and subsequently plundered by the Goths. Still more magnificent than its predecessor, it counted as one of the Wonders of the World.

In our modern conception of things, the site of a temple would be determined in the first place by the architects in consultation with officiating priests or donors. To the ancient Greeks such a notion would have appeared quite inadequate, since a temple site could be chosen *only* by the deity in question. Indeed, the character of the surrounding landscape was inseparably bound up with the nature of the specific god or goddess. Thus, while for the house of Athene, for example, the rocky Acropolis hill overlooking the city of Athens was an appropriate site, the house of Artemis had of a "higher necessity" to be built on low ground, suitable for plants and trees, with a stream flowing westward to the Aegean Sea – despite the presence of a comparable rocky outcrop, the Ayasoluk hill, in the immediate vicinity.

Reporting on a journey to Greece and Turkey in a letter of May 26th 1932, Ita Wegman wrote:

*"... I have enjoyed this trip immensely, and taken into myself the whole of Greece. The ancient wonders affected me like a healing balm and I feel as though reborn and strengthened in continuing to further Rudolf Steiner's work as I bear it in my heart, unwaveringly."*

*"In Greece and Asia Minor we visited the mystery sites of Samothrace, Ephesus, Eleusis, Delphi, Epidaurus (the mystery site of the Asclepion) and many interesting sites of ancient culture and history."*

*"It is certainly important to have visited Greece and these historic sites. Even if one finds nothing more of the ancient mysteries than a pile of ruins, the landscape is still there, and the human heart that had experiences in those ancient times.*

*The contrast between then and now that dawns on one is the incentive for new impulses, if the soul is strong enough to endure it; otherwise one could be cast down by it. In Ephesus the contrast is unspeakable, indescribably great. There Turkish economy and Turkish rule is destroying everything that might possibly still exist. And if one compares the uneducated milieu of today with the one that was once assembled around the Artemision and was inspired by its wisdom, then one could shed bitter tears and be filled with fury and yearn to start another crusade. But what's the good of all that? After all, those connected with the Artemision are in the Anthroposophical Society and even they do not know clearly what is involved, killing what is spiritual cold-bloodedly as well."*

*"The rubble that is to be seen now lies half in a swamp, and we did not shrink from wading through the water so as to reach important places and view them up close ..."* [5]

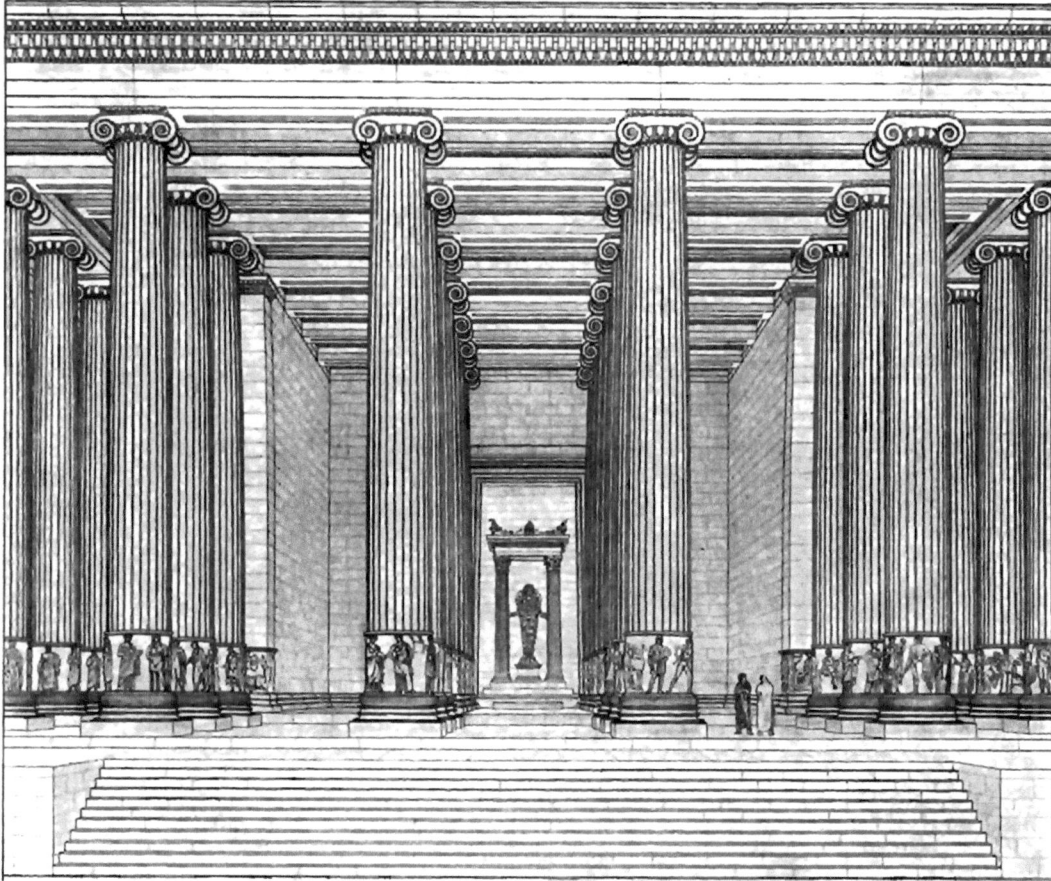

View into the entrance hall of the late classical temple of Artemis.
Reconstruction drawing: *Fritz Krischen*.

The Apollo Temple in Dydima. Open court area with the *naiskos*. (A similar *naiskos* housed the
cult statue of Artemis in the Artemision in Ephesus.) Reconstruction drawing: *Fritz Krischen*.

The entrance hall of the archaic Artemision (built ca. 560-540 B.C.) from the south side
Reconstruction drawing: *Fritz Krischen*, 1946.

The new Artemision was not erected with the intention of following what was by then the current style, as occurred in replacing other temples such as the Parthenon. The aim was to rebuild the venerable sanctuary essentially as it had been. The archeologist *Fritz Krischen* (1881–1949) notes that the ground plan of the old temple was transferred quite exactly to the new one "… so that – as peculiar as it may sound – the axis of the old columns grew up as it were, through the new terrace. For reasons of piety, the stumps of the old columns were not disposed of, but securely packed with stones and then built over." [6]

*Demetrios,* one of the architects of the rebuilding, is said to have been a temple slave of Artemis.
(A. Bammer, U. Muss: *Das Artemision von Ephesos.*)

The second (classical) Artemision, southwest corner. Built ca. 336–310 B.C.
Reconstruction drawing: *Fritz Krischen,* 1946.

On account of the later destruction of the western end of the second Artemision (by earthquakes) the original length of the temple could not easily be determined. Fritz Krischen concluded that there were three, rather than two rows of columns on the west front (see ground plan page 3). With this additional row of eight columns, the overall number (127) reported by Pliny (A.D. 23–79) is duly confirmed. The skepticism of some modern researchers in this regard is shown to be unwarranted. Fritz Krischen bequeathed uniquely masterful reconstruction drawings that vividly depict the ancient historic sites lost to us. The Artemision drawings shown here can be accounted works of art in themselves.

*Underworld Scene.* Marble column drum with relief sculptures. Southwest corner column. (See illus. p. 7.)
Ca. 336 B.C., late classical Artemision. British Museum. Photo: *Frank Teichmann.*

The sculptures depict the gods *Thanatos* (with a sword), *Hermes*, probably *Persephone* and other goddesses. This sole remaining sculpted drum from the late-classical Artemision was discovered 19ᵗʰ September 1871 in the south-western part of the temple.

Though not generally on public display, the British Museum houses an extensive collection of mostly fragmentary archeological finds from the archaic Artemision. No complete archaic sculpted marble drums remain. (The columns were referred to by Pliny as *columnae caelatae*).

In the Greek sculptural tradition of the late-classical period, gods and heroes are portrayed unclothed in mythical scenes, while goddesses appear clothed. No equivalent principle is found in either Assyrian or Egyptian art.

The same column base from the late classical Artemision,
shown opposite, seen from another angle. British Museum. (Photo: *P.St.*)

Tendril woman. Tympanon of the Temple of Hadrian, New Ephesus.
Photo: *Frank Teichmann.*

*In Ephesus the statue of the Gods; here in the Goethe-*
*anum the statue of Man, the statue of the "Representa-*
*tive of Mankind," Christ Jesus. In Him, identifying our-*
*selves in all humidity with Him, we thought to attain to*
*knowledge, even as once in their way, a way that is no*
*longer fully understood by mankind today, the pupils of*
*Ephesus attained to knowledge in Diana of Ephesus.*

Rudolf Steiner, GA 233

## The Cult Image of Artemis Ephesia

The mythical birthplace of Artemis is a secluded grove called *Ortygia* ("quail haven") [7], a sacred precinct in the hills near Ephesus, with a stream running through it. Every year on the 6th of May (zodiacal sign of Taurus), there was a festive procession to celebrate the birth of the goddess along the *Processional Road*, the ancient coastal road connecting her temple with her birthplace.

Daughter of Zeus and the goddess Leto, and twin-sister of the sun-god Apollo, Artemis – one of the twelve Olympian gods – was venerated as a Greek moon-goddess and regarded as a goddess of childbirth. Portrayed on the Greek peninsula as a maiden huntress, she was associated with the forest and especially with the endless wilderness, with untouched Nature. Artemis is depicted holding a golden bow, from which she shoots silver arrows; conversely, Apollo holds a silver bow and shoots golden arrows. Diana was identified with Artemis by the Romans.

The wooden temple statue of Artemis, annihilated and hence unknown today [8] may have somewhat re-sembled small gold or ivory figurines (see illustrations) found on the site of the Artemision. Hellenistic-Roman marble representations of the Mystery cult statue portray a *xoanon* consisting of a basic wooden image of the goddess, furnished with a robe, a bronze *ependytes* (apron), fruit and flower-chains or girdles, as also "half-figures," winged mythical beasts and wild animals. Not depicted in full, but as though truncated, they appeared thus to clairvoyant sight in emerging from the cosmic ether. [9] Never fully entering into the world of appearances, such half-figures are comparable to the mythical "blossom-" or "creeper women" with vines, indications of the after-life, such as can be seen on the temple of Hadrian in the Hellenistic-Roman city of Ephesus (see illustration, page 9).

With its manifold and unique embellishments, the Artemis Ephesia counts as one of the most significant and mysterious statues of antiquity. It has been convincingly demonstrated that the attributes that for centuries were viewed as being multiple breasts – though plainly below breast level – depict bulls' testes affixed to the cultic image of the goddess at festival times following a sacrificial slaughter. [10]

The "non-festival" temple statue of Artemis would have been much simpler, corresponding for instance to one said to have been the work of *Endoios*, a pupil of *Daidalos*. This statue is known to have been at the same time the first cult statue of Artemis with forearms and hands extended. To learn what stood behind such a composite image of the goddess required study going beyond ordinary knowledge. Included was the conception of Artemis as active within all processes of coming-into-being and passing-away. For the seeker after knowledge, or neophyte, "mere knowledge" had to pass over into experience, involving lengthy inner preparation. In the preliminary stages, entailing speech exercises, the pupil took part in what was known as the "Lesser Mysteries."

The nature of the Mysteries practiced at Ephesus, held in strict secrecy, can be surmised from sayings of the Greek philosopher and sage *Heraclitus* (535–475 B.C.), who spent his life in close proximity to the Sanctuary of Artemis. His written work *Concerning the World's Becoming*, in three parts, is said to have consisted of a single copy placed in the Artemision, implying that only initiates fully understood his "secret, holy language." – *"All things are in flux"* was a celebrated utterance of Heraclitus; *"The soul is akin to the Logos, that increases itself;" "We are and are not." "Man's daemon* [that within him which reaches beyond himself] *is his destiny."*

Rudolf Steiner indicated that hearing also played a significant part in the "Greater Mysteries" at Ephesus. It can be shown that for the ancient world, the speech organ (larynx) relates to the zodiacal sign of Taurus and to the forces proceeding from it. There is a sense in which the formative-forces leading to physical existence via procreation and the formative-forces that develop the powers of the human spirit can be seen as analogous. [11]

The training path in Ephesus had ultimately as its aim to lead to an experience of the Logos, of the Cosmic Word.

*"Every aspect of the service to the goddess of Ephesus, known exoterically as Artemis, was designed to give an experience of the creative spiritual forces pervading the cosmic ether. When the participants in the Mysteries approached the statue of the goddess, they had the sensation of hearing her speak, in words such as*

this: 'I delight in all that bears fruit within the vast cosmic ether.'

To hear the goddess thus express her heartfelt delight in everything that grows, buds, and sprouts within the cosmic ether was a truly profound experience. Indeed, the spiritual atmosphere of Ephesus was aglow with heartfelt sympathy for all budding and sprouting things. The Mysteries there were instituted in such a way that nowhere else could one find such sympathy with vegetative growth, with the budding and sprouting of the earth into the plant world." [12]

Thus the main festival of Artemis took place in Ephesus in the spring.

"This Mystery had in the very middle of its sanctuary the image of the goddess Artemis. When we look today at depictions of the goddess Artemis, we have perhaps only the grotesque impression of a female form with many breasts. This is because we have no idea how such things were experienced in olden times; and it was the inner experience evoked by these things that was all-important. The pupils of the Mysteries had to go through a certain preparation before they were conducted to the true centre of the Mysteries. In the Ephesian Mysteries the centre was this image of the goddess Artemis. When the pupil was led up to the centre, he became one with such an image. As he stood before the image, he lost the consciousness that he was there in front of it, enclosed in his skin. He acquired the consciousness that he himself is what the image is. He identified himself with the image. This identification of himself in consciousness with the divine image at Ephesus had the following effect. The pupil no longer merely looked out upon the kingdoms of the Earth that were round about him — the stones, trees, rivers, clouds and so forth — but when he felt himself one with the image of Artemis, he received an inner vision of his connection with the kingdoms of the Ether. He felt himself one with the world of the stars, one with the processes in the world of the stars. He did not feel himself as earthly substance within a human skin, he felt his cosmic existence. He felt himself in the etheric." [13]

A small gold statue of a goddess (ca. 12.5 cm). 7th century B.C., from the site of the Artemision. Ephesus Museum, Selçuk, Turkey.

A small ivory statuette of a goddess (11,7 cm). Ca. 560 B.C., from the site of the Artemision. Archaeological Museum, Istanbul.

Artemis statue. 520 B.C. (1,22 meters).
Plaster of Paris. Colour reconstruction by Vincenz
Brinkmann (2004) employing the same mineral
and earth pigments as used by the Greeks, such as
*malachite* (green), *cinnabar* (red), *yellow ochre* (yellow).
Glyptothek, Munich. Original marble statue, Acropolis
Museum, Athens. (Photo: *P.St.*)

Bronze statuette of Artemis as a huntress,
holding a bow in her left hand
and (originally) an arrow in her right hand.
Around 520 B.C., provenance S. Peloponnese.
Boston Museum of Fine Arts.

Artemis originally held a bow in her left hand and an arrow
in her right hand.

This small figurine corresponds closely to the larger statue
to the left.

Cult image of Artemis of Ephesus. Marble statuette (68,5 cm).
1st century B.C., Museum of Antiquities, Basel, provenance Asia Minor.

Characteristically Greek rather than Roman, this is the earliest Mystery cult image of Artemis that has come down to us. Her distinctive forms ask to be deciphered.
"Identifying himself with this statue which was fullness of life, which abounded everywhere in life, the pupil lived his way into the Cosmic Ether. With the whole of his inner feeling and experience, he raised himself out of mere earthly life, raised himself up to the experience of the Cosmic Ether." (Rudolf Steiner, GA 233, Lecture IV, 27th Dec. 1923.)

Artemis Ephesia (1.74 meters).
Marble statue, Ephesus Museum, Selçuk, Turkey

A copy of the cult statue from the time of Hadrian (ca. 125 A.D.), so-called "Beautiful Artemis". To the right and left, the goddess is accompanied by two hinds. In her hand she originally held a woven woolen cord, of which only the two tassels remain below, also referred to as *omphaloi* (navels). The statue is known to have been decorated with gold. The goddess has carved figures of the zodiac as pectoral ornaments, while her *ependytes* (apron) includes winged mythical beasts.

Monumental marble statue of the Ephesian Artemis
(2,92 meters). 2nd century A.D.,
the so-called "Great Artemis".
Ephesus Museum, Selçuk, Turkey.

The Artemis Ephesia, 17 A.D., Alabaster and Bronze.
National Archaeological Museum in Naples.

This and the statue shown on p. 14 were discovered, to-gether with a third smaller marble statue of Artemis, in the Hellenistic-Roman city of Ephesus in 1956. They originally stood in front of the Prytaneion (city hall). All three statues are in the Ephesus Museum in Selçuk, Turkey.

The crown ("polos") of Artemis is possibly in the form of a beehive (see Hella Krause-Zimmer). The bee was an emblem of Ephesus. Priestesses of the goddess were called "bees".

## The Artemis Ephesia in Naples

A striking feature of this Naples statue from the time of Caesar Tiberius is the contrast of the translucent, honey-coloured alabaster and the dark bronze of the face, hands and feet. The art historian Hella Krause-Zimmer draws attention to the essential difference between the front and the back of the statue:

*"In contemplating the riddles to be solved in con-nection with Artemis, it may easily be forgotten that one is actually only looking at the goddess from the front, and is unfortunately unable in many cases to see more. With few exceptions she is installed in museums in such*

a way that her back remains inaccessible and can hardly be surmised from the side only. One has to make do with a facade, with more or less just one viewing angle. This enhances the strangeness and probably the attraction of the sculpture, and in a sense its power to shock. The viewer thinks he knows the Ephesian Artemis, and yet does not. In going around the statue, he would be in for something of a surprise.

At the back there are no more images, no animals, no signs or symbols. There is no zodiac, no necklace that continues. The "armor plating" [the ependytes, or apron] is not cylindrical and does not continue all around as one would otherwise have to assume; it ends, leaving the back region free. The flat disc of the aura turns out to be a wonderful domed shape. Soft channels and folds in the veil lend the figure a calm beauty. It becomes apparent that the delicate pleating over the feet is in fact an extension of this garment, a subtle indication of what is to be seen at the back of the Ephesia.

Looking at the goddess in this way, she is comparable to a veiled Isis. As "Ephesia" she has folded back her head-covering, and shows on her miraculous figure, motifs that are a revelation of her Mystery. [14]

The Ephesian Mysteries, true harbingers of anthroposophy and at the same time of the art impulse of Rudolf Steiner, come to expression in the following verses:

*Offspring of all the worlds, thou clothed in light,*
*Empowered by the Sun with Luna's might,*

*Endowed art thou by Mars' creative ringing,*
*And Mercury's swiftness, agility bringing.*

*Illumined by wisdom from Jupiter raying*
*And by Venus's beauty, grace bestowing –*

*That Saturn's ancient spirit-inwardness*
*Unto the world of space and time thee hallow!* [15]

Artemis statue. Naples.

Artemis statue. Naples. (Rear view)

## Annotations

1. Rudolf Steiner, GA 233 (lecture V, 28th December 1923)
2. Rudolf Steiner: *World History and the Mysteries in the Light of Anthroposophy.* GA 233, Lecture V, 28th December 1923.
3. „Some readers may reflect on the events surrounding the first and second Goetheanums. One fundamental difference is that Rudolf Steiner conceived the second building as an entirely new creation. Here we are concerned with a „young" impulse, with a still inexhaustible potential for new forms. Nonetheless, it is interesting that Rudolf Steiner initially attempted in his first model to erect the new building over the terrace of the first Goetheanum, which had been spared by the fire." (Hella Krause-Zimmer in *Artemis Ephesia*, 1964.)
4. In his book on Ephesus, Hans Gsänger also names *Scopas* and ten further prominent Greek sculptors, as also six painters who worked on the second Artemision.
5. From a letter to Fried Geuter (and "for all friends at Sunfield.") © Ita Wegman Institut, CH-4144 Arlesheim
6. Fritz Krischen: *Weltwunder der Baukunst in Babylonien und Jonien*, p. 62.
7. F. Teichmann: *Die griechischen Mysterien*, p. 87. (Regarding the house of Mary, above *Ortygia*, see p. 136-142.)
8. History relates that in 406 A.D., Bishop *Chrysostomos* had the temple statue of Artemis, carved out of wood and black from centuries of anointing with oil, burnt, believing that he was performing work "pleasing in the sight of God." Rudolf Steiner points out, much was lost or destroyed in the first Christian centuries.

   "… in the frightful devastation which befell those times. If we look penetratingly at those late Greek sculptures, held on the one hand to be so great, and rightly so, because they point to something, but on the other hand wrongly so, because they are mere imitative reproductions – if we look through them, back to their origins, then we see that in earlier Greek times images of what manifested in the sacrificial rites came into being in the very way I have described, in fact in a much more majestic and magnificent manner than later on." (Rudolf Steiner, *Mystery Knowledge and Mystery Centres*, GA 232, 12ᵗʰ lecture, 21ˢᵗ Dec. 1923.)
9. This is set forth more fully in Frank Teichmann's posthumous work *Die Griechischen Mysterien* (2007).
10. See Gérard Seiterle. „Artemis – die grosse Göttin von Ephesos", in the periodical *Antike Welt*, issue No. 3, 1979, Mainz. (The author grew up the son of a butcher and came in this way to his discovery. He became director of the Museum of Antiquities in Basel.)
11. Hence the two *omphaloi* (navels) of the "Beautiful Artemis" (p. 14) – indicating the interconnection of physical and spiritual birth. See also F. Teichmann, *Die Griechischen Mysterien,* p. 125.
12. Rudolf Steiner, *Mystery Sites of the Middle Ages*, CW 233a, lecture of 22 April 1924.
13. Rudolf Steiner: *World History and the Mysteries in the Light of Anthroposophy.* GA 233, Lecture III, 26th December 1923.
14. Hella Krause-Zimmer, *Artemis Ephesia*, Verlag Freies Geistesleben, 1964.
15. Rudolf Steiner, *The Easter Festival in the Evolution of the Mysteries*, GA 233a, Lecture of 22nd April 1924.

## Literary Sources

Bammer, Anton / Muss, Ulrike, *Das Artemision von Ephesos*, Verlag Philipp von Zabern, Mainz am Rhein 1996.

Gleich, Sigismund v., *Mysteriendämmerung und Christuserscheinung*, Stuttgart 1952.

Gsänger, Hans, Ephesos, *Zentrum der Artemis-Mysterien*, Novalis Verlag AG, Schaffhausen 1974.

Hoenn, Karl, *Artemis, Gestaltwandel einer Göttin*, Zürich 1946.

Keil, Joseph, *Ephesos, ein Führer durch die Ruinenstätte und ihre Geschichte*, Wien 1957.

Krause-Zimmer, Hella, *Artemis Ephesia*, Verlag Freies Geistesleben, Stuttgart 1964.

Krischen, Fritz, *Weltwunder der Baukunst in Babylonien und Jonien*, Verlag Ernst Wasmuth, Tübingen 1956.

Miltner, Franz, *Ephesos, Stadt der Artemis und des Johannes*, Wien 1958.

Muss, Ulrike (Hrsg.), *Die Archäologie der ephesischen Artemis. Gestalt und Ritual eines Heiligtums*, Phoibos Verlag, Wien 2008.

Pfleiderer, Edmund, *Die Philosophie des Heraklit von Ephesus im Lichte der Mysterienidee*, Berlin, 1866.

Romer, John und Elizabeth, *The Seven Wonders of the World*, 1995.

Scherrer, Peter (Ed.), *Ephesus. The New Guide.* Translated by L. Bier and G.M. Luxon. Revised edition 2000.

Seipel, Wilfried (Hrsg.), *Das Artemision von Ephesos*, Verlag Phoibos, Wien 2008.

Steiner, Rudolf, *Mystery Knowledge and Mystery Centres*, GA 233a, Rudolf Steiner Press, UK.

———. *Christianity as Mystical Fact*, Anthroposophic Press, Spring Valley, New York, 1986, GA8.

———. *World History and the Mysteries in the Light of Anthroposophy*, GA 233, Rudolf Steiner Press, London (1997).

Teichman, Frank, *Die griechischen Mysterien*, Verlag Freies Geistesleben, Stuttgart 2007

# About the Author

Born in Copenhagen, Denmark in 1941, Peter Stebbing attended Waldorf Schools in England. Having studied at art schools in Brighton and London, he emigrated to the United States in 1966, continuing his studies at Cornell University and earning the M.F.A. degree in painting in 1968.

While teaching design and colour courses over a period of six years in the City University of New York, he began a practical exploration of the scientific colour phenomena set forth by Goethe in his colour theory. This led eventually to a turning point – to the crucial question of finding a corresponding approach to colour in painting.

The new and wholly different training in colour experience begun in 1976 with the painter Gerard Wagner on the basis of Rudolf Steiner's motif sketches, resolved fundamental artistic questions with a coherent and systematic approach. Fully in accord with Goethe's discoveries and method, this approach may be termed "Goetheanistic."

Peter Stebbing subsequently established a painting school at the Threefold Educational Foundation in Spring Valley, N.Y., teaching there from 1983 until 1990. Since 1992 he has been director of the Arteum Painting School in Dornach, Switzerland. He is also the translator and editor of various anthroposophical art publications.

## *Other Books translated and edited by Peter Stebbing*

- Margarita Woloschin, *The Green Snake. An Autobiography.* Floris Books, 2010. 431 pages paperback.

- Elisabeth Wagner-Koch and Gerard Wagner, *The Individuality of Colour. Contributions to a Methodical Schooling in Colour Experience.* 2nd edition. 128 pages. Hardcover. Rudolf Steiner Press, 2009.

- *The Goetheanum Cupola Motifs of Rudolf Steiner. Paintings by Gerard Wagner.* 236 pages. Hardcover. SteinerBooks, 2011.

- *Conversations about Painting with Rudolf Steiner. Recollections of Five Pioneers of the New Art Impulse.* 195 pages, 77 illustrations, hardcover. SteinerBooks, 2008.

- *Three Grimms' Fairy Tales. Paintings by Gerard Wagner.* 70 pages with 31 colour plates, hardcover. SteinerBooks, 2012.

- Rudolf Steiner, *The World of Fairy Tales.* 23 black-and-white shaded drawings by Gerard Wagner. 124 pages, paperback. SteinerBooks 2013.

- *The Art of Colour and the Human Form: Seven Motif Sketches of Rudolf Steiner: Studies by Gerard Wagner.* 218 pages, hardcover. Verlag des Ita Wegman Instituts, 2017. Also available from SteinerBooks, Great Barrington, USA.

## *Online Activities*

- *On-line [Search](#) of Bn/GA# 190 texts*
- *On-line [Compare](#) of Bn/GA# 190 texts*
- *Rudolf Steiner Archive & e.Lib:  Bn/GA# 190 [Overview page](#)*
- *Wikipedia: [Rudolf Steiner](#)*

# Notes

www.ingramcontent.com/pod-product-compliance
Lightning Source LLC
Chambersburg PA
CBHW041428090426

42741CB00002B/89